GORP
Trail Mix

Jeanne Ulrich

ISBN: 057809620X
ISBN-13: 9780578096209
Library of Congress Cataloging-in-Publication Data
Ulrich, Jeanne
GORP: Trail Mix

First edition, 2012

Published by Charles Ulrich Company, Inc.
info@charlesulrichcompany.com
www.charlesulrichcompany.com

Charles Ulrich Company, Inc.
P.O. Box 3377
Federal Way, WA 98063

To Mom and Dad,
Thanks for my most excellent childhood adventures!

CONTENTS

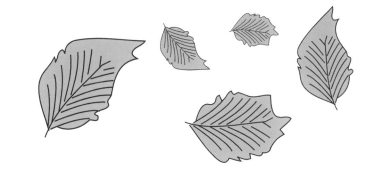

Mount Rainier National Park | Washington

Mount Rainier National Park, established in 1899, has the greatest single-peak glacial system in the United States. The summit and slopes of an ancient volcano create the base of this beautiful mountain that last erupted in the 1800s.

National Park Service (NPS) / NPS photo by Daniel Keebler | For additional information visit: www.nps.gov/mora

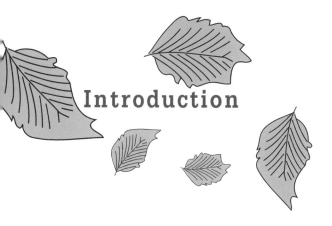

Introduction

Thank you for giving back to help our great outdoors....when you purchase this book you are also helping with the stewardship of our great outdoors. With each book sold a portion of the profits are cycling back to organizations that are leading the stewardship movement to educate, maintain, and preserve our great outdoors—so that current and future generations may continue to create their own most excellent outdoor adventures.

The beautiful photos of America's National Parks featured in this book are from the National Parks Service (NPS) website. To view the NPS online photo portfolio please visit their website at: www.nps.gov – the website offers a "search" feature for finding parks within the United States which is a great way to find parks in areas you are interested in visiting. Additionally, if you click into the "Photos & Multimedia" section you can find photo galleries, multimedia presentations, and virtual tours, along with webcams that allow you to see what is going on in real-time.

I have had the pleasure of working this past year in an environment that cherishes our relationship with the outdoors. It has been a wonderful opportunity to be in the midst of those who are actively pursuing their personal outdoor adventures. What I have come to appreciate is the common love and respect for the outdoors that comes in all varieties: cycling, hiking, fishing, boating, camping, snow sports, and picnics in the park. What's your favorite outdoor adventure?

Badlands National Park | South Dakota

Badlands National Park contains the world's richest epoch fossil beds, dating back over 28 million years. Erosion over hundreds of thousands of years helped to carve a landscape of multicolored canyons, creating an extraterrestrial-like landscape.

National Park Service (NPS) / NPS photo by Rikk Flohr | For additional information visit: www.nps.gov/badl

GORP

GORP is an acronym for "Good Old Raisins and Peanuts" and is often referred to as trail mix. Trail mix usually starts with GORP ingredients and builds from there. The ideas for the GORP recipes in this book were inspired from everyday foods that we all love, such as banana walnut bread and apple pie.

These GORP trail mix snacks are great on their own, but I would encourage you to also try the sweet versions sprinkled on ice cream, cereal, salads or yogurt. The spicy or savory GORP snacks are great to sprinkle on salads or soups and they also pair well as an appetizer with your favorite wine or beer.

These snacks are simple and quick to put together; so cook up some delicious GORP trail mix to help fuel you on your next outdoor adventure.

Visit us online at: www.GORPtrailmix.com

Carlsbad Caverns National Park | New Mexico

Carlsbad Caverns National Park features approximately 113 caves beneath the surface of the desert. These caves were formed when sulfuric acid dissolved the surrounding limestone; the photo above is from a lower cave tour.

National Park Service (NPS) / photo by NPS | For additional information visit: www.nps.gov/cave

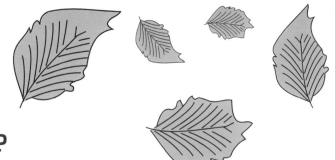

BANANA WALNUT GORP

This GORP will remind you of the flavors of banana walnut bread with just a hint of maple syrup spread on it. Try the Maple Banana Walnut GORP sprinkled on yogurt or on top of French vanilla ice cream.

Directions

1 teaspoon ground cinnamon

2 tablespoons maple syrup

1 cup roasted and unsalted peanuts

1 cup walnut halves

1 cup raisins

2 cups unsweetened freeze dried banana slices or dried banana chips (Traders Joe's has a great selection)

Preheat oven to 300°F.

Line a cookie sheet with parchment paper.

In large mixing bowl combine cinnamon, maple syrup, peanuts and walnuts. Stir to coat nuts evenly.

Spread nut mixture in a single layer on cookie sheet.

Bake 15 to 18 minutes, stirring three times during baking process. Nuts are done when most of the maple syrup has been absorbed and the nuts are lightly toasted.

Set cookie sheet onto wire rack to cool.

When nut mixture has cooled completely, mix with raisins and banana slices.

Store GORP in an airtight container. Best if eaten within a few days.

Servings: 10 | Yield: Makes about 5 cups

Sequoia National Park | California

Sequoia National Park is the second oldest park in the United States, featuring immense mountains, rugged foothills, deep canyons, vast caverns, and the world's largest tree.

National Park Service (NPS) / photo by NPS | For additional information visit: www.nps.gov/seki

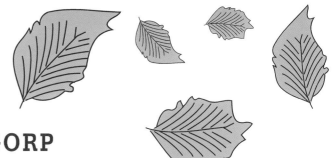

BLUEBERRY VANILLA GORP

Blueberries and vanilla make a wonderful flavorful backdrop to the regular peanuts and raisins in GORP. This recipe also works great to substitute 1 cup of almonds for 1 of the cups of peanuts.

½ cup sugar

2 tablespoons butter

2 teaspoons vanilla

2 cups roasted and unsalted peanuts

1 cup raisins

1 cup whole dried blueberries

Directions

Place a piece of parchment paper on a cookie sheet.
Place butter into a large non-stick skillet over medium heat to melt.
Once butter is melted lower heat to medium low and add the peanuts and sugar. Cook while stirring and turning peanut mixture with a spatula until the sugar melts and turns a golden brown, about 7 to 10 minutes.
Remove from heat and quickly stir in the vanilla (be careful as vanilla bubbles and splatters a bit when you add to the hot peanut mixture).
Pour hot peanut mixture onto parchment lined cookie sheet to cool completely.
When peanut mixture has cooled completely, mix with raisins and dried blueberries.
Store GORP in an airtight container. Best if eaten within a few days.

Servings: 8 | Yield: Makes about 4 cups

Grand Canyon National Park | Arizona

The Grand Canyon National Park is known for its enormous stretch of canyon that is 277 river miles long, up to 18 miles wide, and a mile deep.

National Park Service (NPS) / photo by NPS | For additional information visit: www.nps.gov/grca

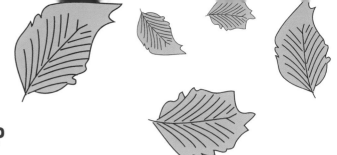

CHERRY BANANA GORP

I was inspired to create this GORP when I was enjoying a bowl of Ben and Jerry's ice cream. This GORP is delicious as a topper for yogurt or vanilla ice cream.

Directions

1 tablespoon ground cinnamon

1 tablespoon sugar

2 tablespoons simple syrup

1 cup roasted and unsalted pecan halves

1 cup roasted and unsalted peanuts

½ cup raisins

½ cup dried cherries

1 cup dark chocolate M&Ms®

1 cup unsweetened freeze dried banana slices or dried banana chips (Traders Joe's has a great selection)

Preheat oven to 300°F.

Line a cookie sheet with parchment paper.

In large mixing bowl combine ground cinnamon, sugar, simple syrup, peanuts and pecans. Stir to coat nuts evenly.

Spread nut mixture in a single layer on cookie sheet.

Bake 15 to 18 minutes, stirring three times during baking process. Nuts are done when lightly toasted.

Set cookie sheet onto wire rack to cool.

When peanut mixture has cooled completely, break up any large clusters and then mix with raisins, cherries, banana chips and M&Ms®.

Store GORP in an airtight container. Best if eaten within a few days.

Servings: 10 | Yield: Makes about 5 cups

Yosemite National Park | California

Yosemite National Park is located east of San Francisco in the Sierra Nevada and is best known for its waterfalls. The park includes almost 1,200 square miles of deep valleys, grand meadows, ancient giant sequoias, and a vast wilderness area.

National Park Service (NPS) / photo by NPS | For additional information visit: www.nps.gov/yose

CINNAMON GLAZED GORP

This is close to a traditional GORP recipe that usually includes peanuts, raisins and M&M's®. The flavor differentiator is the cinnamon and sugar spices that are cooked into the peanuts. These peanuts are good enough to eat alone; you might want to make up a batch of just the peanuts as they make a great topping for salads.

Directions

2 teaspoons ground cinnamon

1 cup sugar

2 teaspoons vanilla

¼ cup water

2 cups roasted and unsalted peanuts

2 cups raisins

2 cups M&M's®

In large non-stick frying pan combine peanuts with cinnamon and sugar. Add the vanilla and water and stir. Place pan on medium heat, stirring often throughout the cooking process. Once the mixture has begun to boil reduce heat to medium low and continue to cook until the liquid evaporates, about 5 to 8 minutes.

Pour hot peanut mixture onto a parchment lined cookie sheet to cool completely.

When peanut mixture has cooled completely, mix with raisins and M&M's®.

Store GORP in an airtight container. Best if eaten within a few days.

Servings: 12 | Yield: Makes about 6 cups

Yellowstone National Park | Wyoming, Montana, Idaho

Yellowstone is America's first national park, established in 1872. The park spans Wyoming, Montana, and Idaho. It is home to a variety of wildlife, including grizzly bears, wolves, bison, and elk. Old Faithful and other extraordinary geysers are popular visitor sites at the park.

National Park Service (NPS) / photo by NPS | For additional information visit: www.nps.gov/yell

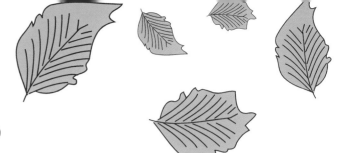

COCONUT BERRY GORP

This Coconut GORP pairs equally well with macadamia nuts or cashews. The flavor of the coconut baked with the nuts seems to bring out a nuttier flavor that lends perfectly to the sweet-sour flavors of the berries.

Directions

1 teaspoon ground cinnamon

2 tablespoons honey

1 cup dry-roasted salted macadamia nuts

1 cup roasted and unsalted peanuts

1 cup sweetened flaked or shaved coconut

½ cup raisins

⅓ cup dried cherries

⅓ cup dried cranberries

⅓ cup dried blueberries

Preheat oven to 300°F.

Line a cookie sheet with parchment paper.

In large mixing bowl combine cinnamon, honey, peanuts, macadamia nuts (or cashews) and coconut. Stir to coat nuts evenly.

Spread nut mixture in a single layer on cookie sheet.

Bake 15 to 18 minutes, stirring three times during baking process. Nut mixture is done when lightly toasted.

Set cookie sheet onto wire rack to cool.

When nut mixture has cooled completely, mix with raisins, cherries, cranberries and blueberries.

Store GORP in an airtight container. Best if eaten within a few days.

Servings: 9 | Yield: Makes about 4 ½ cups

Arches National Park | Utah

Arches National Park features a landscape of contrasting colors, landforms, and textures carved by millions of years of geologic history.

National Park Service (NPS) / photo by NPS | For additional information visit: www.nps.gov/arch

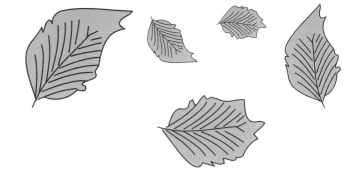

ESPRESSO BEAN **GORP**

This GORP is simple to make and great to munch on for a quick pick-me-up when you can't get to your favorite espresso stand.

Directions

¾ cups sugar

¼ cup water

2 cups roasted and unsalted peanuts

1 cup chocolate covered espresso beans

Place peanuts, sugar and water in a 2 quart glass microwave safe dish, stir.

Place in microwave - total cooking time in microwave on high setting is 8 to 9 minutes or until the sugar has caramelized. You will need to stir several times during the cooking process.

Pour out the hot peanut mixture onto a parchment lined baking sheet to cool. When completely cooled, break into small clusters.

Combine cooled peanut clusters with chocolate covered espresso beans.

Store GORP in an airtight container. Best if eaten within a few days.

Servings: 6 | Yield: Makes about 3 cups

Hot Springs National Park | Arkansas

Natural Hot Springs water has drawn visitors for more than two hundred years to this park. The park collects the water from the hot springs and distributes it to the public via a row of historic bathhouses.

National Park Service (NPS) / NPS photo by Gail Sears | For additional information visit: www.nps.gov/hosp

GINGER SPICE DELIGHT GORP

If you are a fan of ginger then this GORP would be a great snack to take along on your next outdoor adventure...and it is great to sprinkle on soups and salads.

½ cup sugar

2 tablespoons butter

1 teaspoon vanilla

2 teaspoons dried orange zest

2 cups roasted and unsalted peanuts

2 cups raisins

¼ cup diced crystallized ginger

Directions

Place a piece of parchment paper on a cookie sheet.

Place butter into a large non-stick skillet over medium heat to melt.

Once the butter is melted lower heat to medium low and add the peanuts and sugar to pan. Cook while stirring and turning peanut mixture with a spatula until the sugar melts and turns a golden brown, about 7 to 10 minutes.

Remove from heat and quickly stir in the vanilla and orange peel (be careful as vanilla bubbles and splatters a bit when you add to the hot peanut mixture).

Pour hot peanut mixture onto parchment lined cookie sheet to cool completely.

When peanut mixture has cooled completely, mix with raisins and ginger.

Store GORP in an airtight container. Best if eaten within a few days.

Servings: 8 | Yield: Makes about 4 cups

Joshua Tree National Park | California

Joshua Tree offers a fascinating variety of wildflowers, world-class rock-climbing, and surreal geologic land and rock formations caused by climatic extremes.

National Park Service (NPS) / photo by NPS | For additional information visit: www.nps.gov/jotr

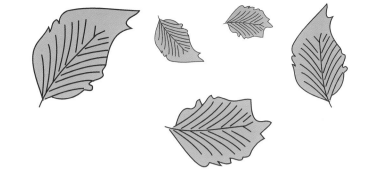

INDIAN CURRY GORP

These spicy and savory GORPs are great as a snack and also work well as an appetizer served with wine or beer. This Indian Curry GORP tastes great as a topping for salad or soups.

¼ teaspoon ground cardamom

¼ teaspoon ground ginger

¼ teaspoon garlic powder

¼ teaspoon red pepper flakes

1 teaspoon curry powder (use hot curry powder if you want more heat)

¼ cup sweetened flaked or shaved coconut

1 tablespoon olive oil

2 cups raw Spanish peanuts (can substitute regular raw peanuts)

2 cups raisins

1 cup dried banana chips

Directions

Preheat the oven to 250°F.

Line a baking sheet with parchment paper.

Place cardamom, ginger, garlic power, red pepper flakes, curry power, coconut and olive oil in large bowl, add peanuts and toss together until peanuts are completely coated with the spices and oil.

Transfer the peanut mixture to the lined baking sheet.

Spread out the peanut mixture into a single layer.

Place in oven to bake. Total baking time is 40 to 45 minutes; you will need to stir the peanut mixture every 15 minutes while baking.

Remove from the oven, place baking sheet on wire rack to cool.

When peanut mixture is cool stir in raisins and banana chips.

Store GORP in an airtight container. Best if eaten within a few days.

Servings: 10 | Yield: Makes about 5 cups

Haleakala National Park | Hawaii

Ancient and modern Hawaiian culture comes together in this park that is home to endangered species, stark volcanic landscapes, sub-tropical rain forest, and beautiful backcountry hiking.

National Park Service (NPS) / photo by NPS | For additional information visit: www.nps.gov/hale

MACADAMIA PINEAPPLE GORP

This GORP has a tropical appeal that will make you dream of sunny days by the water. Try the Macadamia Pineapple GORP sprinkled on yogurt or on top of ice cream.

Directions

1 teaspoon ground cinnamon

2 tablespoons honey

1 cup dry-roasted salted macadamia nuts

1 cup roasted and unsalted peanuts

1 cup raisins

1 ½ cups dried pineapple chips – I like the Trader Joe's vacuum fried pineapple chips

Preheat oven to 300°F.

Line a cookie sheet with parchment paper.

In large mixing bowl combine cinnamon, honey, peanuts and macadamia nuts. Stir to coat nuts evenly.

Spread nut mixture in a single layer on cookie sheet.

Bake 15 to 18 minutes, stirring three times during baking process. Nuts are done when lightly toasted.

Set cookie sheet onto wire rack to cool.

When peanut mixture has cooled completely, mix with raisins and pineapple chips.

Servings: 9 | Yield: Makes about 4 ½ cups

Acadia National Park | Maine

Acadia is located on the rugged coast of Maine and attracts enthusiasts of water sports such as kayaking and canoeing. The park is home to the tallest mountain on the U.S. Atlantic coast and was the nation's first national park east of the Mississippi.

National Park Service (NPS) / NPS photo by John Chelko | For additional information visit: www.nps.gov/acad

ORANGE CRANBERRY GORP

The pecans and cranberries in this GORP remind me of the flavors we see during the holiday season – you might want to make an extra batch or two and put in glass containers wrapped with a festive ribbon as a great holiday gift.

Directions

- 1 teaspoon ground vanilla bean
- 1 teaspoon dried orange zest
- 2 tablespoons maple syrup
- 1 cup pecans
- 1 cup roasted and unsalted peanuts
- 1 cup raisins
- 1 cup dried cranberries

Preheat oven to 300°F.

Line a cookie sheet with parchment paper.

In large mixing bowl combine ground vanilla bean, dried orange peel, maple syrup, peanuts and pecans. Stir to coat nuts evenly.

Spread nut mixture in a single layer on cookie sheet.

Bake 15 to 18 minutes, stirring three times during baking process. Nuts are done when most of the maple syrup has been absorbed and the nuts are lightly toasted.

Set cookie sheet onto wire rack to cool.

When peanut mixture has cooled completely, break up any large clusters and then mix with raisins and cranberries.

Store GORP in an airtight container. Best if eaten within a few days.

Servings: 8 | Yield: Makes about 4 cups

Glacier National Park | Montana

Glacier National Park is known for its forests, alpine meadows, rugged mountains, and spectacular lakes. The park is a hiker's paradise with more than 700 miles of trails.

National Park Service (NPS) / photo by NPS | For additional information visit: www.nps.gov/glac

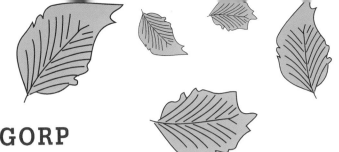

PEPPERED PISTACHIO **GORP**

If you love the taste of pepper then this is the GORP for you. This GORP makes a great appetizer to serve with wine or beer and is also good sprinkled on a salad.

Directions

½ cup sugar

2 tablespoons butter

1 tablespoon freshly ground (medium) black pepper (use up to 2 tablespoons of black pepper for a stronger flavor)

1 teaspoon kosher salt

2 cups roasted and unsalted peanuts

1 cup raisins

1 cup dry roasted, unsalted, pistachios

Place a piece of parchment paper on a cookie sheet.

Place butter into a large non-stick skillet over medium heat to melt. Once butter is melted lower heat to medium low and add peanuts and sugar.

Cook while stirring and turning peanut mixture with a spatula until the sugar melts and turns a golden brown, about 7 to 10 minutes. Remove from heat and stir in pepper and salt.

Pour peanut mixture onto parchment lined cookie sheet to cool completely.

When peanut mixture has cooled completely, mix with raisins and pistachios.

Store GORP in an airtight container. Best if eaten within a few days.

Servings: 8 | Yield: Makes about 4 cups

Olympic National Park | Washington

The Olympic National Park is a nature lovers delight with Pacific Ocean beaches, rain forest valleys, glacier-capped peaks, along with a spectacular variety of animals and plants.

National Park Service (NPS) / photo by NPS | For additional information visit: www.nps.gov/olym

POMEGRANATE DARK CHOCOLATE GORP

This GORP is quick to make and the pomegranate and dark chocolate is a great combination.

¾ cup sugar

¼ cup orange juice

1 cup roasted and unsalted peanuts

1 cup walnut halves

1 cup dried pomegranate seeds

1 cup raisins

1 cup dark chocolate M&M's®

Directions

Line a cookie sheet with parchment paper.

Place peanuts, walnuts, sugar and orange juice in a 2 quart glass microwave safe dish, stir.

Place in microwave - total cooking time in microwave on high setting is 8 to 10 minutes or until the sugar syrup is very thick and is coating the peanut mixture. You will need to stir several times during the cooking process.

Pour out the hot peanut mixture onto a parchment lined baking sheet to cool. When completely cooled, break into small clusters.

Combine cooled peanut clusters with M&M's®, pomegranate seeds and raisins.

Store GORP in an airtight container. Best if eaten within a few days.

Servings: 10 | Yield: 5

Grand Teton National Park | Wyoming

The Grand Teton National Park is known for its spectacular landscape, majestic mountains, pristine lakes, and extraordinary wildlife.

National Park Service (NPS) / NPS photo by Sarah Zenner | For additional information visit: www.nps.gov/grte

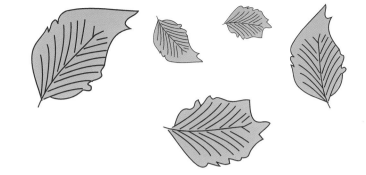

PUMPKIN SEED **GORP**

This GORP reminds me of the fall season when we start seeing pumpkins in the stores for Halloween. Pumpkin Seed GORP is also great to use as a topping for salads and soups.

Directions

2 teaspoons pumpkin pie spice

½ cup sugar

2 tablespoons butter

1 cup roasted and unsalted peanuts

1 cup roasted pumpkin seeds

2 cups raisins

Place a piece of parchment paper on a cookie sheet.

Place butter into a large non-stick pan over medium heat to melt. Once butter is melted lower heat to medium low and add the pumpkin pie spice, sugar, peanuts and pumpkin seeds.

Cook while stirring and turning peanut mixture with a spatula until sugar melts and turns a golden brown, about 7 to 10 minutes.

Pour hot peanut mixture onto a parchment lined cookie sheet – sprinkle with ½ teaspoon salt (optional). Cool completely.

When peanut mixture has cooled completely, mix in raisins. Store GORP in an airtight container. Best if eaten with a few days.

Servings: 8 | Yield: Makes about 4 cups

Fire Island National Seashore | New York

Fire Island National Seashore is known as a special place with dynamic barrier island beaches, high dunes, and ancient maritime forests. Photo above is from the boardwalk trail through the salt marsh and dunes at Watch Hill.

National Park Service (NPS) / NPS photo by P. Valentine | For additional information visit: www.nps.gov/fiis

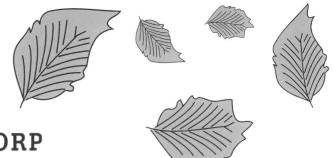

RUM GLAZED APPLE GORP

This Apple Rum GORP is a delicious treat on its own and pairs well as an appetizer with a selection of sharp cheddar cheeses.

¼ cup sugar

¼ cup dark brown sugar

¼ cup dark rum

1 cup roasted and unsalted peanuts

1 cup pecan halves

1 cup raisins

1 cup dried apple pieces

Directions

Preheat oven to 300°F.

Line a cookie sheet with parchment paper.

Place sugars and rum into a large non-stick skillet over medium heat. Cook while stirring until sugar has melted, about 5 minutes.

Add the pecans and peanuts to the pan, stir well to coat nuts.

Pour hot peanut mixture onto parchment lined cookie sheet. Spread nut mixture in a single layer.

Bake 15 to 18 minutes, stirring three times during baking process. Nuts are done when lightly toasted.

Set cookie sheet onto wire rack to cool.

When nut mixture has cooled completely, separate any large clusters and mix in the raisins and dried apple.

Store GORP in an airtight container. Best if eaten within a few days.

Servings: 8 | Yield: Makes about 4 cups

Great Smoky Mountains National Park |
Tennessee, North Carolina

The Great Smoky Mountains National Park is world renowned for its diversity of plant and animal life, along with the beauty of its ancient mountains.

National Park Service (NPS) photo by NPS | For additional information visit: www.nps.gov/grsm

SMOKEHOUSE MAPLE GORP

This GORP has a wonderful smokehouse maple flavoring that is great as a snack or appetizer, but it also pairs well to sprinkle on top of a baked potato or salad.

Directions

1 tablespoon McCormick's Grill Mates® Smokehouse Maple Seasoning

2 tablespoons maple syrup

1 cup roasted and unsalted or lightly salted cashews

1 cup roasted and unsalted peanuts

1 cup raisins

Preheat oven to 300°F.

Line a cookie sheet with parchment paper.

In large mixing bowl combine Smokehouse seasoning, maple syrup, peanuts and cashews. Stir to coat nuts evenly.

Spread nut mixture in a single layer on cookie sheet.

Bake 15 to 18 minutes, stirring three times during baking process. Nuts are done when most of the maple syrup has been absorbed and the nuts are lightly toasted.

Set cookie sheet onto wire rack to cool.

When peanut mixture has cooled completely, break up any large clusters and then mix with raisins.

Store GORP in an airtight container. Best if eaten within a few days.

Servings: 6 | Yield: Makes about 3 cups

Rocky Mountain National Park | Colorado

The Rocky Mountain National Park is a living showcase to display the grandeur of the Rocky Mountains, with elevations from 8,000 feet in the grassy valleys to over 14,000 feet at Longs Peak.

National Park Service (NPS) photo by NPS | For additional information visit: www.nps.gov/romo

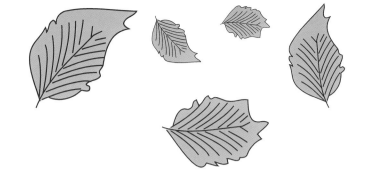

SOY GLAZED GORP

This GORP has a delicious soy glaze cooked into the peanuts, it is great as a snack and also can be served as an appetizer or sprinkled on a salad or soup.

Directions

3 tablespoons soy sauce

2 tablespoons sugar

1 cup roasted and unsalted peanuts

1 cup walnut halves

1 cup raisins

1 cup wasabi green peas (crunchy snack variety)

Preheat the oven to 250°F.

Line a baking sheet with parchment paper.

Place soy sauce, sugar, walnuts and peanuts in a large bowl, stir well

Transfer the peanut mixture to the lined baking sheet.

Spread out the peanut mixture into a single layer.

Place in oven to bake for 10 minutes, stir nut mixture and raise oven temperature to 300°F and continue baking for another 5 to 10 minutes, until nuts are golden.

Remove from the oven, place baking sheet on wire rack to cool.

When peanut mixture is cool, add in raisins and wasabi green peas.

Store GORP in an airtight container. Best if eaten within a few days.

Servings: 8 | Yield: Makes about 4 cups

Crater Lake National Park | Oregon

Crater Lake has inspired people for hundreds of years with its beautiful lake, sheer surrounding cliffs, and a violent volcanic past.

National Park Service (NPS) photo by NPS | For additional information visit: www.nps.gov/crla

SPICY AND SWEET GLAZED GORP

This spicy and sweet glazed GORP has an incredible flavor and while it works great as a snack, you might also want to set it out as an appetizer.

¾ cup, plus 2 tablespoons sugar

2 tablespoons butter

1 cup roasted and unsalted peanuts

1 cup walnut halves

½ teaspoon ground cumin

½ teaspoon medium grind black pepper

¼ teaspoon cayenne pepper

1 cup raisins

Directions

Preheat oven to 300°F.

Place a piece of parchment paper on a cookie sheet.

Mix together a spice mixture of 2 tablespoons sugar, ground cumin, black pepper and cayenne pepper, set aside.

Place ¾ cup sugar into a large non-stick skillet over medium heat, stirring constantly until sugar has become liquid and is light in color, about 8 to 10 minutes. Add in butter and stir mixture until butter is melted.

Remove from heat and stir in peanuts and walnuts.

Spread nut mixture in a single layer on cookie sheet.

Bake 15 to 18 minutes, stirring three times during baking process. Nuts are done when lightly toasted. Remove from oven and sprinkle with spice mixture.

Set cookie sheet onto wire rack to cool.

When peanut mixture has cooled completely, break into pieces and mix with raisins (Note: make certain to include any of the spice mixture that is left on the cookie sheet too).

Store GORP in an airtight container. Best if eaten within a few days.

Servings: 6 | Yield: Makes about 3 cups

Bryce Canyon National Park | Utah

Bryce Canyon National Park is noted for its unique geology of red rock spires and horseshoe-shaped amphitheaters.

National Park Service (NPS) photo by NPS | For additional information visit: www.nps.gov/brca

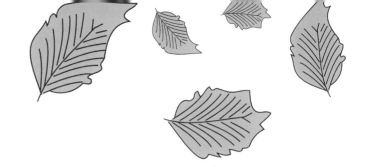

SPICY CAJUN GORP

This Spicy Cajun GORP was inspired by a love of New Orleans food. This is a great GORP to set out as an appetizer as it pairs well with wine and beer.

Directions

¼ teaspoon ground ginger

½ teaspoon garlic powder

¾ teaspoon cumin

1 teaspoon Tabasco sauce

1 teaspoon hot paprika

1 tablespoon Worcestershire sauce

2 cups roasted and unsalted peanuts

2 cups raisins

1 cup sweetened shaved or flaked coconut

Preheat the oven to 300°F.
Line a baking sheet with parchment paper.
Place ginger, garlic powder, cumin, Tabasco, paprika and Worcestershire sauce in a large bowl, add peanuts and toss together until peanuts are completely coated with the spices.
Transfer the peanut mixture to the lined baking sheet.
Spread out the peanut mixture into a single layer.
Place in oven to bake. Total baking time is 15 to 18 minutes; you will need to stir the peanut mixture every 5 minutes while baking.
Remove from the oven, place baking sheet on wire rack to cool.
When peanut mixture has cooled, add in raisins and coconut.
Store GORP in an airtight container. Best if eaten within a few days.

Servings: 10 | Yield: Makes about 5 cups

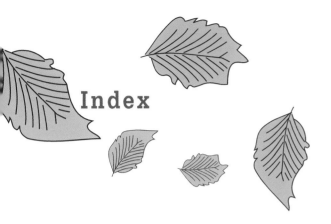

Index

About the Author

Jeanne Ulrich is grateful to be living the dream; with work, home, and family in the Pacific Northwest. She has sailed the San Juan Islands, ridden her motorcycle on beautiful backcountry roads, and had the privilege of visiting many of the parks featured in this book. As a child, Jeanne took many road trips with her grandma Lucille that included visits to some of these wonderful parks—certainly a bucket list would include the opportunity to visit many more of our national parks.

Made in the USA
Charleston, SC
12 April 2013